Salt Lick

Photograph by William Stafford.

SALT LICK
A Retrospective of Poetry

Glenna Luschei

WEST END PRESS

Most of the poems in this collection have appeared elsewhere, both in periodicals and in other collections by the author. Poems that appear here for the first time in a collection are credited below. Magazines in which these poems have appeared are credited at the back of the volume. A list of the author's own volumes of poetry and related collections is also included at the back of the volume.

Poems appearing here for the first time in a collection:

"Not Quite Love" was published in *Pembroke Magazine.*
"The Beautiful Game" was published in *Finalmente: Brazilian Poems by Hugh Fox* (Solo Press Chapbook Series 4, 2007).
"He Called Me Oatmeal Protestant" was published in *Eating the Pure Light: Homage to Thomas McGrath* (Backwaters Press, 2009).
"A Pereira" was published in the anthology *How Luminous the Wild Flowers* (Tebot Bach, 2003).

First edition, February 2009
Paperback 978-0-9753486-9-7

Special thanks to Bill Witherup as contributing editor

Book and cover design by Nancy Woodard
Cover painting, *Catron County*, by Susan Kelly
Back cover photograph by Nell Campbell

For book information, see our Web site at www.westendpress.org.

West End Press
PO Box 27334
Albuquerque, NM 87125

For my sons Erich and Tom Luschei

Contents

all really short lines

Preface

"I live by runes not rules," the poet Glenna Luschei has written. "I told my boss the last time/I got fired/Somehow I get by/dashing from beauty to beauty" [from "Principal"]. Indeed she does, and she has provided plentiful beauty to help others get by, too, not only as a writer but also as a translator, a scholar, a publisher and catalyst. Poet James Bertolino calls her "one of the great spirits of literary community."

Luschei, "a corn detassler and bean walker as an Iowa high school student" who later studied at the Iowa Writers' Workshop, then served as an editorial assistant to Karl Shapiro at *Prairie Schooner*, started a poetry journal she called *Café Solo* in 1967. "We treated it like a cottage industry," this mother of four recalls, "the kids putting magazines into envelopes and stamping them. My youngest, who was still crawling, used to threaten us by saying 'I tear!'"

Forty years later, thanks to her leadership and willingness to commit personal resources, the journal—now called *Solo Café*—is thriving. That's amazing, since the "litmags" of that time—and small presses, too—have had the life expectancy of ailing may-flies. For Luschei, "It's still fun. It's still rewarding."

The late sixties were, of course, a singular time when rebellion was in the air and freedom of expression was on the rise. A few stalwarts such as New Directions and Swallow Press had "carried the brunt of publishing new poetry in America in the forties, fifties, and early sixties," according to small-press veteran Paul Foreman, but late in the decade an alternative publication tide was rising. Editor Len Fulton recalls that his first edition of the *International Directory of Little Magazines & Small Presses* in 1964–65 contained only 250 listings. By the mid-1990s, the number had risen to 6,000 and today has leveled off at 4,000.

People who weren't there—and some who were—summarize the sixties as "sex, drugs, rock & roll," but others also recall political activism, assertive egalitarianism, and what poet Mel Weisburd calls "the poetry of social consciousness, but in its most lively, passionate, even surrealistic form." Luschei agrees: "The entire national climate was changing, so we had different motives for radicalizing literary expression."

Many writers, editors, and publishers of that time defined themselves in relationship to causes ranging from feminism to environmentalism to stopping the war in Vietnam, and expressed fierce independence from what was perceived as increasingly profit-driven major publishers and "effete" university presses, as well as other manifestations of "the Establishment." Glenna, who had in the early 1960s attended congressional hearings on the Civil Rights Amendment, says, "I think my consciousness was . . . connected with civil rights and equality."

Not until 1967, when she and her family returned from a sojourn in Colombia where her first book, *Carta al Norte*, had been published and where the depth of poverty had stunned her, did she determine to start her own review in order to introduce the work of Colombian writers to the United States. Unfortunately, "it was as if the mail service went out of existence. I couldn't get them to send me poems." Nevertheless, *Café Solo* sputtered to life, then thrived.

During this time, Luschei met Weisburd and Gene Frumkin, co-founders of a defining Southern California literary magazine, *Coastlines*. Impressed, they "encouraged and guided her to get involved with publishing activities." She recalls "that the scrapbook appearance of the alternative press was a landmark revolution. The idea was that anybody could be a publisher."

After Glenna was published by George Hitchcock in *Kayak*, she wanted to create a magazine as lively and as professional as his. In those days of dittoed, mimeoed and—if one was lucky—photo-offset publications, she was also determined to produce "an artistically appealing magazine" that would invite readers. Most of all, *Café Solo* "was meant to be a stimulant, coffee without any cream or sugar. I wanted it straight and black, to get rid of some of the overadorned poetry that we still saw published forty years ago."

As an editor, Luschei judiciously mixed the work of established writers with that of promising newcomers. She still favors that formula, as well as concentrating on individual themes such as women's writing, Latino voices, and "Immigration: How We Came to this Country." Of the latter she explains, "We . . . wanted people to tell their life stories. . . . We have poems of people coming here from all over Europe, South America, and Asia, with stark memories."

Being an editor, she soon learned, was different but not necessarily less demanding than being a writer. As a poet herself, one who had endured rejection, Glenna was reputed from the start to bring an unusual sensitivity to authors of unaccepted work. Lisa Steinman, editor of *Hubbub* and now a poet of note, recollects that as an undergraduate at Cornell she had submitted material to *Café Solo*.

> The poems came back (as most poems did), although with a sweet letter. I thought nothing more about it until—perhaps a year later—I received, unsolicited, a letter from Glenna, who said she had made a copy of one of the poems I'd sent her, continued to think about it, and decided she wanted to publish it. A young writer, I was thrilled but had no idea how unusual it was to find an editor or publisher who attended so seriously to poems, who might carry one around with her and reopen the question of supporting a new and naive poet's work.

Steinman concludes by calling Luschei "a model for poetic community and generosity."

Shortly after founding *Café Solo*, Glenna and her family moved from Albuquerque to San Luis Obispo on California's central coast, where she soon became an important cog in the literary community. "I do identify with the central coast because of its rural emphasis," she later reflected. She also found the poetry scene there "harmonious . . . because we have the common cause of protecting our habitat."

After the second issue of *Café Solo*, Luschei was invited by George Garrett to participate in a literary conference at Hollins University in Roanoke. There she met future Pulitzer Prize winner Henry Taylor, and when she returned to California decided to publish a book of the promising poet's work, so she created Solo Press. Taylor's *Breakings* in 1971 was its initial offering. Two years later she printed May Miller's *Not that Far*, followed by future Poet

Laureate Ted Kooser's *A Local Habitation & a Name* in 1974. Some forty titles now constitute Solo's list, with Scott Barrett's *Dosage* in 2006 a recent release.

Glenna's own poems, twenty-one books and chapbooks from many different presses, continue to be written in original styles and to be sent all over the world, revealing an eclectic mind with enduring passion for a variety of people and places and conditions. In "Thaw," for example, she writes of the natural world:

Herons, plovers
mat the rush

Ponds unseal a nest.

The Rio Grande stretches legs
out of winter.

In "Divorcee" she writes of human nature:

Why call the divorcee
promiscuous?
She's only a spruce
putting out cones in a drought.
Under threat of extinction
we all reproduce. . . .

Obviously, she finds both natures interesting and worthy.

Three decades after founding *Café Solo* (and publishing in it such distinguished poets as William Stafford, Denise Levertov, John Berryman, Thomas McGrath, Josephine Miles, and W. S. Merwin), Glenna "realized that the idiom had changed. Language had developed to a truer level in my opinion, and we no longer had to publish a stimulant without cream and sugar." She charged two younger poets, Jackson Wheeler and David Oliveira, to recreate the journal as *Solo*; they would edit, she would publish. The three decided "we would not publish editors or reviewers of our magazine for the express purpose of avoiding cronyism."

With the name change, "the magazine became *Solo*, more mainstream but still, we hope, still singular." Gifted writers such as Wilma Elizabeth McDaniel, Billy Collins, Gary Young, Robert Bly, Naomi Shihab Nye, and Dixie Salazar, among many others, contributed poetry as varied and surprising as one might hope for, leading another poet, Adrianne Marcus, to observe that the editors "brought a high standard that other poetry magazines might want to emulate: better-known magazines have nowhere near the thrust of language that *Solo* has."

Along the way Glenna, now living with her second husband on an avocado ranch down California's coast at Carpinteria, became the first female board member of COSMEP, the Committee of Small Magazine Editors and Publishers, and later its chair. She also served for four years as a panelist for the National Endowment for the Arts and never flinched from community activism.

She developed, for example, Solo Flight, the cultural activities offshoot of Solo Press. It took a number of forms: architects in town talking about their dream structures; poetry and jazz festivals with Ferlinghetti, Rexroth, and Ernest Gaines in attendance. Gwendolyn Brooks came to Cal Poly with our support. We had a Portable Theatre, and Mural Artists: Painters and Students (MAPS). We sponsored a poetry radio program, the Raven Show.

Under the aegis of yet another of her projects, India Inc., neighborhood arts centers were opened in San Luis Obispo and Atascadero. Writer Michael Harris explains such prodigious energy and creativity: "She never lost her playfulness"—and she seems to prove that a playful mind is apt to be an innovative one.

But those things don't fully summarize Luschei's accomplishments: along the way, she won a National Endowment for the Arts Fellowship, a D.H. Lawrence Fellowship, and an Ethel Fortner Literary Award. She also earned an MA, then a PhD in Hispanic Languages and Literatures from the University of California, Santa Barbara, and she taught everything from poetry to papermaking at California Men's Colony, a state prison in San Luis Obispo, as well as at nearby Atascadero State Hospital. Dorothy Stafford writes, "A snapshot in my mind's album is of Glenna getting out of her trusty BMW beautifully dressed (was she wearing a hat?) and entering a dark prison to teach creative writing to the prisoners."

Perhaps most notably, at the seventy-fifth anniversary celebration and conference for *Prairie Schooner* at the University of Nebraska in 2001, she announced the Luschei Endowment to support the magazine in perpetuity. As James Bertolino observes, "She demonstrates there is no inconsistency between art and communal experience."

After seven issues of *Solo*, David Oliveira left for Cambodia and Glenna decided to take a sabbatical from publishing. She carries herself lightly and with grace, but Luschei's life has by no means been breezy. She has endured divorce, the demise of her mother, and the almost unbearable death of one of her children. In *Pianos Around the Cape*, published in 1999 by Apermont Press, she dealt with loss tenderly and without self-pity:

> In my airport dream
> I see you passing through security
> with your excellent posture.
> You carry my blue suitcase.
> I release that baggage now.
> We're both pilgrims,
> both safe. I send up my poem to grief.
> (from "My Last Poem to Grief")

Following that sabbatical year, Glenna relaunched her magazine in 2005 as *Solo Café*. This time Elizabeth Carmo and Kevin Patrick Sullivan served as editors, while Glenna remained the publisher. "I wanted it to be just for fun, for rejoicing in the coffee houses with our sisters and brothers," she explained. But fun and rejoicing were by no means the only purposes of the journal. In fact, *Solo Café* 2, published earlier this year, was dedicated to "Oppression and Forgiveness." Edward Field's "Down in the Valley" served as the foreword of that issue; he did not mince words:

> . . . Poets! Come down from the safety of the mountain
> into the valley of death and destruction,
> to help the innocent
> and say what needs to be said.

Most successful alternative presses and journals survive due primarily to the vision and energy of one person but, paradoxically, that person is often adept at creating community. When Luschei reports that Solo Press and *Solo Café* are "still a cottage industry," you can bet the cottage contains some enthused colleagues, since she has continued networking, encouraging, and nurturing.

As a poet who is a publisher and editor, she has demonstrated artistic freedom and has rewarded originality; no "my way or else" for her. Playwright Len Berkman has pointed out that "Glenna [has] directed the ardor of her words not toward soliciting interest in her own artistic output but toward the embrace and support of others' artistry." That generosity of spirit has characterized her press and her magazines and, as a result, Glenna has become, according to Mel Weisburd, "the center of an important literary network up and down the state."

In *Solo Café* 2, California's Poet Laureate, Al Young, begins "You Do all This for Love" this way:

> You make me cry. You do all this for love.
> You do it all because you dare to care,
> you dare to dream. Someone has to act.
> You're sick of hearing about how somewhere
> over the rainbow. . . .

While Glenna hasn't necessarily found the pot of gold, she has found the love and respect of many fellow authors. Forty years down the road, she points out, "It is the duty of the small press to confront the establishment. . . . We are the canaries in the coal mine." And in her case, the canary remains a pretty fair singer.—Gerald Haslam, Penngrove, California

El Mar

El Mar: the crash of the name
makes me want to flee Bogotá.
The maroon tile rooftops,
the cold mountains
with emerald lights,
the stone houses brown in the rain.

How can we escape?
No lights, gas, water, car.
We are in bondage
to the ferryman of Amazonas.

I want to descend into the flowers,
to feel the tropics closing around me
as the emerald enfolds its garden.

I want to curl out at last on warm sand,
to roll in the pink and orange
hollow of the caracole.

At the top of my senses
I watch for my deliverance
like the New Bedford woman
at her widow's walk
or mad Carlota spying
from the castle her
French emperor trotting
toward the palace of Mexico.

Colombia

Rain on the golf course
brings out the mushrooms.
Our mad tea party
in a misty country,
waterfalls and fungus
and a prehistoric fern
still creeping.

I get the feeling
we're being watched.
Things we leave out
are gone by morning.

Golden locust
hinged in the vaults:
Are the assaults
directed by the Conquest?
Are we the next victims
of the dwarves with wickets?

Beyond the green
there lies the lost city
of insects.
We will know of violence,
dark archeology
on the living.

Among the Rushes

Odor of roots of zinnia
curled head over heels
in a green glass
cracks my memory.

Going back.

I sleep underwater
barely holding the lifeline,
tangled in the rushes of dreams
we left with sea horses.

Already my child is learning
terrors I would keep from him.
My poor drowned nurse is here,
somewhere beneath the drawbridge.

The sleepy days will soon be over.
Then the largeness,
then the birth,
then the milk wires through the breast.

Dream of Snow

The winds hum through icicles.
This is where the thistles blow,
this is where the souls go
to listen to the flute.

I will rattle the pods.

I cannot see through the milkweed.
I cannot reach the blizzard.
Why am I here?
Have I come to sing for my father?

Hold
the opal of my heart
until it warms.

Back into My Body

My mother is dying.

I give her a bath—she's pregnant
with death
swollen belly and one nipple gone
where I bit down as a baby.

I'm taking her back into my body.

My mother is pulling silk
from the cocoon
not to lose the thread.
She's larva again.

She's taken her hands
from my shoulders
no longer yells
"Straighten up!"
Death has come to take her back
and only the well
pass blame.

Worms are at work in her veins.

***

Only the beautiful
hide their breasts and you

naked as a spool
have arranged the linens
for one last time
and touched the cranberry glass.

In the fight for your antiques
leave me nothing.
I'm alive
and strong with you back in my spine.
I lift you from your bath

and dry
and love you.

Anniversary Poem

On the outside
this house is all smiles.
See the poppies blow north?
Inside,
the goldfish
are down at the mouth
while the toy soldier
walks stiff-legged
right out the door.
This is a broken home.

There was a mother
who cried into her pillow
until storks carried her off.
Then the children ate
what was left
and each went a separate way.
North, South,
East, West.
Wait!
Is it only a crossword?

If the Caliph of Dawns
pronounces,
we can roll up the tongue
of the sidewalk
with the snails
and slugs, poppies,
kids,
soldier, father,
mother,
and stick them inside by morning
leaving only the windmill
hitching a ride to Fresno.

Wheat Straw

The tractors plowed me
under
the deep gray loam

with shreds of pottery
and arrowheads.

Gone

my yellow hair
that sang to the trawlers.

The Pozo Basket

I wove this basket
from arrow grass
to cook
the fish that you would bring.

The other women knew
that you would not be back.

Wove it from tule
and bound it with pine gum;
other women knew
that you would not be back.

I lifted rocks from the fire
with oak sticks
and placed them in my basket
to cook the acorn mush
to cook the fish that you would bring.

I loved you
who took me lightly.

Visitations

The probation officer saves the
hardest question until last:
"Do you have men coming through
your bedroom door?"

Oh, don't you know that
they are ghosts
who slide through our shutters
and crack open our pain?

And if you're watching
these visitations
at my bedroom door,
Sir,
shouldn't you instead follow the fog
as it rises with herons
over the lake?
Can't you catch on to a ladder of legs
and drift to rookeries
where the poor in heart can rest?

Jesus said,
"Take care of my sheep."
During the day if I feed each one
and don't refuse the bleating
for help
aren't my nights my own?
Don't I own my sliding-glass pane
and the ghosts and the men?

Do we all drift
to each other at night to whisper,
"Let me love you right while we're still alive?"
I've dressed myself in fog and wool
to tell you we are joined.

Fires at the Station

Tonight is kingfisher time.
        —Lynn Strongin

Our nest has always rested on the wave
and killdeer screamed to mates at midnight watch
while neighbors slept.

Waste and wind and ruin
are songs the cast-iron bells
of the stones
of the marriage temple sing.

He pours the Almaden down the sink
I saved for rock cod stew.
We made our nest
trusting no wind to ruin.

In the first year of the temple
he smashed the Steuben glass
gave away my skates
my puck
my hockey stick
and my fur-lined cape

to the Goodwill.
(Grant me some in telling this tale.)

And when the children's cherry syrup
gurgled
down the drain
my mother's voice surged up to me
La la loo
leave him and save yourself.
Hitch kingfishers to your sleigh
come home for Jesusmass.

Run with your babes in your greatcoat
before archers
strike you down.
My dear did you know
such a long time ago. . . .

Mother, that song
of robin redbreast, orphans in the snow?

Waste.
How can I make it good?
Is dance the only thing?
Mother, your story of Nijinsky's foot
with tendons of a bird.
Did he fly away
in his opera cape,
face music in Ukraine?

Can I dance and spring the robins?
Ballon and leap, plié.
My mother's voice hums from the drain,
sorrow into joy.

When Frey sleighed to Odin
to rescue the winter queen
did *he* try to melt *her* down?
(Oh good will
and armies of salvation
tonight *is* kingfisher time).

Light me the fires at the station
we'll dance in Petersburg.
The time between Christmas and New Year's
I'll wind a week-long nest.
We're all emigrants.
Nothing is lost when you dance.

Chevrolet

Let him keep
the Encyclopedia.
       —Lawrence Ferlinghetti

Though I'm driving around
with my clothes in the back
of my Chevrolet
and my blouses flap through the breeze
and one shoe is lost
and I'm getting divorced,
one half of the soul is free.

It once was community property—
Yes dear, whatever you think—
but now it's my own
and I can fly
flapping clothes in my Chevrolet.

Though he rips me off
when I glide out
and steals the encyclopedia,
if we're measured by what we do without,
my wingspan can only increase.
My half of the soul
gets freer each day,
sing the clothes in my Chevrolet.

Redwoods
for Betty Spaulding

You walk with me through redwoods.
The sun aims knives
through shafts of pine
to strike crystal in the fern.
You say, "When I was young
I cleaned your cut-glass bowl
the one for cranberry sauce.
I scoured it with sawdust."

When I was young
my chore was dusting the redwood plaque
above the davenport.
Trains pulled into the lumberyard
unhitched planks and two-by-fours.
Sometimes families lived in boxcars.
Father brought them food.
O, to hop a freight train out to Portland.

Near the edge of the forest
we find a fallen nurse-tree
growing laurel from its bark.
We discover goose pens—corrals
of burnt-out trunks
where settlers tethered goats.
We carry home a geode,
crystal at its heart.

You remember settlers
from seventy-five Thanksgivings;
I hike with a pioneer through these giants
who thrive even without their heartwood.
In spite of lightning and fungus
they grow up and up
two thousand years.

Fern Grotto

The river boat steers us
through banks crowded by the hau trees.
In a life of twenty-four hours
their flowers
change colors three times a day.

We float past the thicket of Fili grass
past the swamp where the Chinese grew rice
to the inland harbor of the fern grotto.

I walk behind the waters
into the cave.
I came for a blessing.
Instead I find a band:
ukeleles, guitars, an enormous soprano.

Where do they carve the hau tree canoes
bend the branches for fishing poles?
There still must be a part of me
that comes to life again each day
with the yellow hau flower.

Autumn

Rains reach down
to rough the fur of sand
and men rake sand
instead of leaves.

A woman strides along the shore
in a faded red suit I would hate to wear.
She is no passerby of autumn,
as I am, in my chair.
She is a red memory of a leaf
in a country where leaves never fall.

Tea has come, and while I hold my cup
rain grabs up waves by the neck.
The cup of the horizon fills with sun,
round as a dollar,
sand or silver dollar.

I watch an old man watch the sea
wash out his castles.
He leaves the stars alone with me,
an unexpected grace
that makes me know at last a foreign place
and season.

Day of the Kings

It's as if
you lived in a country
where every night
the family sat around the hearth
and when the children were asleep
the grown-ups went out and
dropped bombs.

And the children wondered:
"When you fill our stockings
why do you drive the others
from their huts?"
And the grown-ups said,
"You don't understand.
This is work."

The children huddled.
"Should we fight our parents?
They own us.
Shall we take over the barn?"

It's as if we lived in a country
where wise men
sighting a star
said, "What splendor!
They're intercepting a missile."

It's as if you were bearing gifts
and couldn't find the foot
of the stall.
No place to lay down
the myrrh.
No way to end.

Inland Passages

Lakes in the Chugach Mountains
flush out in a day.

In one night
the polluted metals of my life
dissolve.
I must show my children
how to walk on mud.

Sun stays up
to forge me into gold
though the moon furls out white
and grand as a Matanuska cabbage.

Juno, stirring up the moon,
are you an alchemist?
Will you let me use your crystal
as crucible through trial?

Aren't you too
cut apart from your mate?
You drift with me through inland passages
from Juneau
to Prince Rupert to Ketchikan
down to the lower forty-eight.

Halloween Dream

One by one the condors
come onto the pine branch
and we shoot them.
Pellets enter pear-shaped bodies.
At the end of the dream
they are extinct
and we mourn.

In the pedal boat out in the lake
we recall the Day of the Dead in Mexico:
children sitting on graves of ancestors
in the churchyard
women in rebozos selling corncakes,
chrysanthemums in candlelight.
Why do we forget our dead?

In the half-light rowing home
we see children set out in Halloween sheets.

Generation after generation
walks over the horizon.
We take our place
single file
on the limb
and month after month
we long for a child.

Throwing away My Shoes in Tokyo

How can I toss these shoes
into the trash?
They carried me to every shrine in Kyoto.

They stood outside inns and bathhouses
faithful as the dog at Shibuya Station
forever awaiting his master.

They protected me on the bullet trains
got muddied while the doctor
wearing rubber boots
showed me where to pick strawberries.

I might have left them at the Shogun's Palace
where the cricket boards chirp
when an intruder approaches the bedchamber.
These shoes sounded warnings.

They were black patent leather,
dressy to the last.

Cedar Waxwing

The cedar waxwing stabs
my pane.
To save him from the cat
I lay him in a cage.

In the morning he is singing,

drunk from sipping
the last of my pyracantha
berries.

Farewell to winter.
I fly on air to the Bahamas.

On the white beach
a fiddler crab with binoculars
reminds me
I forgot sunglasses.

I travel light.
It all fits into a postcard.

Outer Island

The fan turns in my room.
How long it takes to forget a lover.
I must pay my grain bill.

My last child leaves
for an outer island.
Hot noon, the fan
turning slowly.
I have learned nothing
since graduation.

I mustn't be afraid.
Mother looked like an Egyptian queen
in her coffin.

Zombies

Witchcraft: Bury zombies
twenty-four hours
to bring them back to life.

Sweat covers me
like my first skin.

Questions we asked
at the airport
play back from a steel-drum band.

What is the money?
            The dollar.
What is the language?
                  English.
What is the speed of light?

I thrust my lack of trust
into the zombie's grave.

We have all we ever need
traveling light.

We will survive the stabs,
be saved from drunken pain.

I saved the cedar waxwing.

Roads to California

My dream sets anchor in your arms.   I water-ski
behind the moon   skim the Missouri where I waded
as a child.

Though floods whirled up to our back screen, we children
slept buried in sand.   The goose-necked lamp   ran
with the ostrich.

Grain bins blew apart.
The highway swelled with rotting wheat.

From Ventura you wave   cross the berm from creek to lemon
trees.   I wake in the crescent
of your flank.   I first knew the ocean at thirteen.

Tidepools

You told me your name meant dearly beloved.
I said we were friends through all incarnations.

I won't weep your dissolution.
Carry no mourning into tidepools   David   with your lyre
singing.

The Pacific fed our friendship,
        flooded   ebbed.

Time was not a stream running through our hands   not film
through the reel of your projector.

Gone
for a month   a year   always underwater you were David
singing.

Dearly beloved   somewhere in your death   starfish cling
to serpentine   sand dollars crust on the beach.

I Thought They Would Never End

I thought they would never end
the walks through the meadow of the blue vervain
where the heron nested in eucalyptus.

I thought they would always remain
my four blue eggs.

I thought my luck would never end.
I would hoist up one skein of flounder after another.
Loaves would fall into my open hands.
Look.   Oh look.

I think my life will never end.
How lazily I go about it.
Every day will open morning glories.

Can my world stay the same
no boundary wars   no bombings?
I put my teapot on and lose my head again in steam.

Arrangement

It's 110 in Atascadero this July
with poison oleander in full fire.

I try to change the arrangement of this bouquet.
It's perfect but I don't know what it means.
The thistle is as lovely to remember
as the Chinese bellflower.

When I bring together silk and barbed wire
ferns curl about my fingers.
I haven't got a green thumb. I get by.

In Colombia we gave away orchids every day.
A boy sold us cheese. It was round and moist
as the Colombian sun
and wrapped in a banana leaf.
He asked me for flowers in a jar: "I have to bury
my brother, drowned in the arroyo."

Atascadero in Spanish means darkling mire.
I like it here. As I pass the snapdragons, I stop
to give them water.

Jean Seberg

Jean Seberg came from Iowa as I did.
I gained the lead in *Our Miss Brooks*, as Sister Margaret
in *The Hasty Heart*.

Jean did better. Otto Preminger cast her in
The Lark. She played *Bonjour Tristesse*,
married her French lawyer in Trinity Lutheran Church.

Her husband introduced her to Romain Gary, the novelist (consul
general in Los Angeles). She loved Gary and bore his son.

Gary said:
>   You have to understand the
>   midwest. She emerged from it
>   intelligent, talented, beautiful,
>   with the naivete of a child.
>   To me her goodwill is infuriating idealism.
>   It made her defenseless.
>   In the end it came between us.

I love with
too much innocence.

Jean married Gary. While filming *Paint Your Wagon*, she fell in love
with Clint Eastwood, later with Hakim Jamal, assassinated
for betraying the Black Muslims.

Jean wrote to *Liberation*:
>   Hakim Jamal, cousin of Malcolm X, ex-user, convict;
>   the most beautiful man who walked the earth;
>   he's dead my Jamal;
>   eight slugs in the belly,
>   seated in a rocking chair
>   surrounded by family.
>   You killed my Jamal.

Jean became pregnant. The FBI the *LA Times* and *Newsweek*
speculated about the father, rumored "Black activist from California."

Publicity threw her into labor.
A girl was born by Caesarean, named Nina
after Romain Gary's mother. The baby died three days later.

In Marshalltown, they left the coffin open. People could see that Nina
was white.

Gary insisted: "I am the father."

At the Left Bank restaurant Le Medina,
Jean met Algerian Ahmed Hasni.
She started her film, *The Legion Parachutes into Kolwesi.*

After a fight with Hasni, she threw herself onto the Metro tracks; was
pulled to safety.

I prayed for Jean and for those who've pulled me from the tracks.

She wrote to her son:
     "Be good and forgive
     the mama who loves you."
Police found her body in a blanket in the back of her Renault on the Rue
de Longchamps.

Jean was buried at Montparnasse.

Three months later Romain Gary sat at his desk
and put a bullet through his head.

He wrote:
     "No connection with Jean Seberg. Lovers of broken hearts are
     kindly asked to look elsewhere."

To Enter a Greenhouse

We built our canoe
from second-growth ash
and each autumn
chinked the cabin with resin.
The first Thanksgiving since divorce
I swell on reunion.

Unable to bear
this holiday alone,
I take the Greyhound to San Francisco
past boxcars of sugar beets
fields of artichoke and orange asparagus fern
past cauliflower that has more brain
than I do.

Why don't I pursue my studies
or read great books
instead of dwelling on canoes
built from second-growth ash?

I've strained the learning from myself
to care for animals and plants.
The birthing lambs need blankets.
I need touch.

Can what is dissolved
be strained, flushed and restored?
Can we curve the hoop
underwater and rejoin it
in latticework wicker?

This is the season for lambing
for rejoicing in my family.
Before I plant new seeds,
I must consider the harvest.

April in Lincoln

Snow loops a cobweb
through the eaves.

Your love threads my ribs.
Free as a spider
I glide to you.

Linda, my first-born
I delivered you at home
held you in my arms.

See the sun
through the fingers of trees.
This is the church.
This is the steeple.
These are the lilies on the edge of spring!

Visiting Hours

My aunt tells me she's writing a story
just by turning the leaves of the pad.
Beautiful,
not a word on the page.
It's light, pure light.

Against her hospital screen
I sense Nebraska wheat, coast
in the wooden wagon
Grandpa once pulled me in
nights too hot to sleep.
Ants crawled down the peonies.

Our lives grow bound
through every year
by every wind.
I am reading your story.
My heart turns page after page.

Christmas Bread from Verona

Ciao Luigi:

I heard opera in the Baths of Caracalla
bought a stiletto umbrella
and black high heels from the man
who measured my foot with his hand
thirty years ago.

Now *Pandoro di Verona* arrives on Christmas Eve
in a box like a birdcage.
Does the postman think he carries calling birds
or cardinals from St. Peter's?

I bake bread
but it's rye in the form of a toaster.
Your pandoro is golden, light and high.

You sent me the basilica of breads!

I bake the bread and baste the goose
can I return to *Italia bella?*

Snow falls on tombstones of Romeo and Juliet.
I powder sugar over bread from Verona.

Con molto amore,
Glenna

I Want To Be Your Poet

I want to be the poet
who invites you up the sweet-
smelling stairs.
My redwood home
would welcome the traveler,
sun on pine needles,
light through clerestories.

I want to be the poet
who sits through the night with you
cricket calling
    cough of the kit fox
rasp of the newborn word.

I want to be the poet
who will weep with you
when it's time to leave,
who remembers
the burgundy of flowering plum.
Flap, flap.
Blue jay in the birdbath.

I want to be the poet
who can kiss you awake.

I'm not afraid of garlic breath.
I'll deliver CPR.
From your garden I'll pull out the onion
with a head like Einstein.
Get ready for surprise!

I'll whisk you through
the silk & barbed wire.
I want to be your poet, your lover.

Straight Answers

Power in Poetry
begins in secrecy.
—Henry Sauerwein

Everybody begs me:
"Give me a straight answer!"

The 8th of October
I watch the spider
spin a web from its body—
Why can't I be simple?

The 9th
I fly into Albuquerque
through painted balloons
that bellow across the desert.

Here I find answers.

The arced flight of the snow goose
is never straight.
In the burning bush
the voice is heard.

Beneath a raging moon
Karen and I bathe in Japanese hot tubs.
Flying saucer snowflakes skim our heads.

"Trust in the wooden wall,"
the oracle at Delphi said.
I have trusted wood
since I was a child
and kegs of blue nails
like sapphires,
and spiders and their webs.
I trust the word in the desert.
I trust the arc of the snow goose.

Here

Love's in the daily doings
the blister on the first roasting chili
the race to gather sheets
at the wick of lightning.

We fold the linen with lavender
and sage.

Love's the oar that pulls us to the sea.

You propel me over quick
silver waves to San Luis Obispo,
through spidery hills of black oak,
call me home.

The mica I bring you
scatters in my pocket,
but the Hunter's Moon
tracks it to the tarmac.

Why scan the moon's two continents for love?

Our friends shout, "Look around!"

It's here beside us
on the dark side.

We fold the linen with lavender
and sage.

At the Passover Feast

"Too many hands in the kitchen!"
Firemen extinguish the skillet.
I recline against orange blossoms
                              in the garden.
I reach out
to that peach moon.   No Angel
of Death may come here tonight.
What do you see in the moon;
the embryo of life we engender?
A year ago I woke to the alarm.

In my dream
you carried the baby on your shoulders,
wove me through galaxies of wire
                    around your heart.

The Seder promises:
though we are prisoners now,
next year
               we shall be free.

Julie at the Lighthouse

She always wanted to come here.
I saw it windswept and desolate.

How gentle though
the cow-swept clover fields
where the Angus lean like barns.
For her: a cloverland of calves.

The sea horse in my spine
spurs me to the lighthouse
on the beach.
We lie on our backs
dazzled by praying hands of sun.
Our loss ticks away.

With a cut of its wing
pain flies out of my back.
I will ride the horse to the field
and gather the last wreath,
will see Melissa married
beneath the desert willow
and the double rainbow.

Julie will ride the horse to the finish
and receive the wreath.

Bare Root Season

I hit rock bottom.
My shovel strikes boulder
in the creek.

Beneath white sycamores
I reason
if I find no soil
if my shoulders hurt
then my heart must wait.

Plant now
or forever miss the fruit.
Roots can worm their way
through earth.

Darling,
it's the bare root season.

Bare Root

These are unprotected sticks.
Not one leaf. I choose wisteria
to climb the oak,
lift up hearty root-stock
from the peat moss.

It's bare root season.
In this strange land
I yearn for the canopy
of foliage,
yearn for my old home.

Metamorphosis will come for me,
trans-movement through the light.
I will take hold, one day wear
the laurel. I dig, and learn
that I can tether; quick pain
is part of nature.

Elegy for Julie Graham

Trimmers free my giant valley oak
of Spanish moss and mistletoe.
Over axe and saw I hear the drumbeat
from the high school band. Word arrives
from Albuquerque: my friend has died.

Can we call a woman an oak? It's Julie!
She packed adobe bricks by hand, called herself Datura,
Buffalo Woman to friends.
She took my hand when I was new in Albuquerque.
We blessed new homes in Zuni Shalako.

When my son was a baby, I carried him to Julie's adobe.
His hair caught light from her stained glass.
Now he starts his junior year.
Julie sent her stained-glass window, *Burning Bush*,
with me across the desert to the ocean.

Hydraulic chairs lift pruners to the branch
where wisteria flowers in the oak.
I witness the ballet and plead with men to save
the purple bloom. My friend has died
in Albuquerque.

The voice of creation speaks to me, voice
of the artist never consumed, voice of Orpheus.
I hear the drumbeat of old land,
catch the desert scent of creosote bush.
My friend has died.

Men with Their Secret Gardens

There is always a man
who brings me back from Santiago
when I have barely met Gabriela Mistral.
Even at the prison
there is a man who pushes open
the revolving gate.
Door after door.

I carry a man on my coattails
until he conquers me,
undresses me,
saves me in distress.
A man will impregnate me
at the moment I am due to make a discovery.

My champions are men.
I bear sons. They drive me
to the homestead where I climbed
the apricot tree.

When I walk around the block
where I memorized the cracks
picked blue flax
they step on the gas. They honk
when I stop at the library where I checked out
Jo's Boys when I was ten.

Men.
There is always a man to
unlock my cage,

to throw away my papers, to enrage me.
"Man the editor; woman the creator," I wrote.
A man to shoe my horse
a man to operate the buzz saw while I dodge the splinters.
To fund my projects, give me money, take it from me,
steal my daughters.

Men cover our fingers with secret
gardens of emeralds.
I wear the engagement rings of my grandmother
and three aunts. "Engaged."

Do you gain the trust of a heifer
to lead her to a distant place of slaughter?

One day I will take off all my rings
and give them to my grandsons,
never know who will wear sapphires of loyalty
rubies for heart
diamonds forever
only the veins of my hands sprout potato tubers.
I will remember my happiest hours
(after men grow tired of uprooting me)
digging in my own garden.

How Will I Care for this Baby?

"Let me take the phone where the children can't hear."
Over long-distance wire you told me:
    back room of the clinic
    dark for hours,
    tissue scraped from the womb
    oyster
    from the shell;

    I sent flowers.

You called to tell your dream:
    nightmare child
    grew so fast you couldn't hold her.
    How will I care for this baby?
    Who will protect this child?
Your therapist said,
"You will take charge of your own growth now.
You are the baby."

When I stayed in your house
I awoke to midnight shrieks.
A cat?
Coyote? Was it human? Was it you
keening for the baby, La Llorona of legend?

Cortés stole his children
from La Malinche
to send them to Spain.
She asked to say goodbye
led them to the river and with a machete
cut their throats.
The wind still howls across the canyon mouth:
    Who will protect my child?

You invade my home with the passion
of the gypsy moth.
All night I hear your pen
chew paper.
We are torn from the children by your pace:
to the train, to the restaurant,
to the beach.

The baby would be ten. I wish
she had been mine.

A Life in the Garden

They have all passed through me,
passed through the harp of the bleeding heart.
They parted the golden strings.
They chose me.

Unaware, I chose them to live
with me in the grove
and turned down no one.
We knew any moment
the crystal would fall.

The heavy avocado
at the end of its tube:
this was the womb I provided.
I prune the trees on the oblique;
they all chose me.

Is it too late now,
when I speak will they peer beyond me?
When I hiss
will they turn stiff backs?

O, in allowing them room,
the verdulaga with the corn,
did I misuse the garden?

I fed them hemlock. I fed
them rue. The harp sounds the one
true tone.

Injection

In Bogotá where children slept on streets
under bullfight posters
three figures reach out of the dark.

The woman wears herringbone. She touches
my arm. "Señora,
Señora, this is my daughter, and her baby
is sick. Could you give us money?"

I am in my twenties.

I reason—
if I give her pesos
she may buy *aguardiente.*

I take her to the pharmacy
stark with light.
It smells of ether.
The druggist gives the baby an injection.

Years later, I wonder why I didn't ask their story.
Why were they in the street at dusk?

I had to buy meat for my family. I hurried
home to supper.

Bill of Lading

My passport has arrived.
It's time to move on.
I own my books and the dining-room table.
My mother shipped it from Iowa
when they ran the highway
through our house.

Here I ladle Brunswick stew
I learned in North Carolina.
I publish books from this table,
elect the president.

One guest,
Camilo Torres, priest,
brought Marxist students to my house
the night before I left Bogotá.
Possessions stacked in cartons,
I listened for Colombian revolutions.
Waiters in black tie
served champagne.

One month later
I saw Camilo in *La Prensa*
dead
eyes still open.

I can't blame my table for what happened
in the Andes
for the highway through the plains.
Poets write.
Revolutions form.
Hear a baby cry every morning.

Matriarch

Remember when the oak crashed into the roof?
Branches longer than the house
allowed the tree to topple.
That was the November Joseph died.

I tend the Dickinson, tallest avocado
in the orchard.
Head and shoulders above the rest,
it draws me back when I get lost.
We sell fruit
but I preserve the tree for history.

My garden cultivates me, tears me
from my journal. Cymbidium shows its
first spike in January.

Remember when we pulled apart
those tangled veins beneath the oak?
That was the November Joseph died.

I make peace with my mistakes, admit
some things never mend, heal crooked.
I tend the orchard.

repeating words/lines

Safe Deposit Box

In the vault I view the birth
and death certificates, finger
Grandmother's engagement ring,
cavity in the center where the diamond shone.
We picked an acre of iris and peony
every Decoration Day.
(I adored her spotted arms.)

And here's the pistol.
My forebears are buried in Furnas County
where Grandmother defended her brother
against murder charges.
Nebraska's first ballistic test
proved the bullet came
from Grandmother's pearl-handled revolver.

Uncle Ott got off. I've got one remaining bullet.

Grandmother was a great shot
and so was my mother in the days
of Bonnie and Clyde, but I'm the Wing
Walker, witness.
I spirit away the lore
of family gone before.

My son asked me for the diamond for his wife.
My daughter-in-law with eyes
like smoking pistols
wears the stone that traveled across the prairie,
that calmed me in the root cellar
during the tornados.

During those storms
Grandmother sang, taught me to spell.
She won her fifth-grade spelling prize:
the watercolor of Grace Darling.
Grace rowed out to her shipwrecked father.
She saved him from drowning.

I gave that painting to my daughter.

In my family, daughters save the men,
brothers defend the secret.
I lock up the lore of family gone before.

like the sounds

Originals

Karl, we can't believe it now,
but I used to be
your secretary. When Howl

came out you sent congratulations
to Ginsberg.
I took your calm

dictation in my impeccable
Gregg shorthand
then hiked the letter home

for my army clerk husband
to type. I presented the originals
& carbons to you at 9:00 a.m.
clean as a new baby. You said, "Ahem.
Good work." You, handsome
with your white hair, a real poet!

Luckily
I soon had a new baby. You sent me
congratulations.

When I came back you had a real
secretary. You looked guilty.
I cried. You said,

"Howl will change our lives."

Condor Rap

The condor's wings burgeon
beneath my trapezia.
Muscles flex.

    Get out.

Fly over the Andes. Fly over sandy
Antofagasta.

    O condor,

you're a tough baby.
Lady,
when you faced extinction
you flew back
and grabbed what you needed.

Lady,
you're crazy
if you don't follow your breeding.
Aim for the throat.
You're not the Amazonian
Pecho Puñalado,
caged bird with the wounded
heart.

You're grander than the American
bald eagle.
Admit you love carrion.

    Admit

though life is a good chain,
life is a food chain
and everyone wants what you've got.

Everyone wants what you've got,
Old Bird.
The next time they circle
it may be over your delicate
bones.

Burst out, condor, don't look
back.

Water Song

When you climb
Mount Tamalpais
and the squall you view at sea
beats you to your van,
sleet
hits the windshield
in badger prints.
You fall in love with water again.

You forget the blackened Berkeley hills,
friends routed from their burning homes,
the Yukon Express
that froze the groves.

When you catch a band
of grazing mountain sheep,
the rams kick and butt.
You know there will be lambs
in the spring.

When you hear the snowy tree
cricket sing the water song,
you know the High Sierra flows
again after another winter.

Water
in the Merced River,
water over Nevada Falls,
water over Vernal Falls.
In the ancient path of glaciers,
we praise the green hills.

Spirit of Place

I envy the ouzel
her spirit of place.
She sings in the waterfall's
embrace: mossy
                    wet
                        nest.

O envy the ouzel
who lives in the icy stream.
To protect her home
we save willows
though rivers flood the vineyard.

Perched on a mid-stream rock
she bobs up.
She calls *Bzeet.*
Bzeet.

Through the floods we hear her song
while we gain solid ground:
our place to sing.

Untitled

Like Cabeza de Vaca
& Coronado
we searched for gold
in these cities.

We saw the mica
pueblos
in San Ildefonso,
the broken pop
bottles
on the streets
of Taos.

What glittered
was the road.

short lines

Zuni

From a crook in the sky:
Shalakos retreat
to their hills,
done with clacking,
feasting.

Sun, track them, crook
of an eye.

Shadows walk on stilts.

Shiprock

I

I have no telephone,
cables are down in the snow.
Only
the antlers of my pelvis
catch me in.

Still
you have reached me.
Square bales of hay
make me think of your pueblo
and you going about,
a thousand times smaller.

The red tunic!
Your long braid.

II

In the kiva
the beans have sprouted
the Hopis
          chant

My belly
strung
          each breast
the pick of a mandolin.

Taos

Life's short
as the name
of this town
where the mica
pots
and pop
bottle glass
tell us
we've got the gold.

Life's short.
Let's fight.

Carpinteria

I

I plant cosmos
long for galaxies.

Uranus lies
obliquely on the axis.
Natives,
oblique
unique
but lonely,
marry
and bear children.

Welcome to Neptune
with the freezing moons.

II

All night
wind machines whir.
Decades slip away
like eels
out of my hands.

O frost,
fix my thought.

Leave the lemon
yellow
in peace.

Prairie Schooner Poem

The fog settles over us
a brooding
hen.
Oh, how it tucks in the shouting and screaming.

We sit around the table
painting books
and Russian Easter eggs
talk of wolves
white nights on the prairie.

What is it in winter
warms
protects the family?
Iron beds and bunks
draw in together, the baby's cradle
center.
We're secure in prairie schooners;
is the snow circling us like Indian ponies?

Yes.
I'm a snow princess; I've summoned this storm
to offer peace to my dear ones.
See the colors in my prism?
see tonight, the coldest night
brittle gold and crimson?

In the morning
won't frozen cream
pop out the bottle tops?

No.

It's only a childhood dream.
This is California
where trucks carry onions from Salinas,
rooster combs of chili pods.
The grass inside our redwood fence is green
and turning greener.

Cabbage Leaf

The second death
waits through radiance
of broken Persian melons
like moons outside Visalia
past chartreuse rice fields
and Stockton Delta sheep.

Yuba City means:
we're halfway to the Rogue.

We stop at Merlin
for line and flies.
("Ammo and gold pans.")
I wish for magic.
It's true there's no cure.
We've got a year.

We're late in the season,
river dark
from alder berries.
Remember
I taught you to thread
a needle?
Now: check
beneath the cabbage leaf
to find the hatch.
We'll match it with the caddis fly.

⟩ break

We drift
through mist to find the steelhead.
We know the big one
beneath the waters.
He's been to the ocean
and back.
With the taste of salt,
he swims for his life.

When he bites on the fly,
we'll give him line.
After the fight
we'll throw him back.

You say, "I'll never forget."

Next morning
the ice-chest sun barges in.
I weep beneath the Hudson Bay blanket
like an addict.

No Escape

Scorpio moon:
We hose the garden down.
The smell of it,
water on earth.
Long childhood rides in the heady
Iowa evening.
Ford windows wide.

But here.
Death collects salt
water under my house,
spreads out in tentacles.
No escape.
I hold my line together,
let my daughter sleep on.
Grant her health, peace,
water on earth.

Death inches out in leech fields.
Fifty years ago
my aunt bred tangerine trees for the ranch.
We can graft the branches
of the remaining six
onto lemon stock.
We must keep them going.

I brace myself
to say goodbye to the oldest
member of our family
and to my own firstborn.

In the life of this ranch
one crop replaced another,
walnuts to lima beans.
Earth replaces water.

For supper I pick corn
and serve the cracked
box crab.
Deep, deep
claws reach out from coral.
We are eating limestone.
Sleep sprinkles down the house.
Water on earth.
Even in escape
I keep it going.

Kernel

You hung in there, *hung | bat*
kernel before the statue
of Bernardo O'Higgins.

You, out of ten thousand
bull men, rushed Europa.
You were mine.

You hung in there
with a hole in your heart.
That long bus trip,
Chile to Miami.

But every day your heart bled
one or two drops.
I knew I would lose you
as later on I did.

You hung there
like a bat
until you were born.
I took your arms,
slid you to my groin while I
cut the cord.

Little by little
the vampire drew
out your blood
replaced it with bile.
Later on
I lost my child.

Quick

Everyone else sees the dead.
Why don't I?
Why can't you appear
as suicides do
to those they left abruptly?
Sit on the edge of my bed!

You keep beneath the surface,
in my lungs.
Sink or swim, I can't spit you out.

I've got you in the dead man's hold
but always underwater.
Come back just once.
Say, "This has to be quick."

Everyone else hears the dead.
Why don't I?
"Death knocks, but does not enter,"
my grandmother said
and even though she was deaf
she heard the knocking,
heard the procession of ancestors
file by her grandmother's coffin
in the front door, out the back.

That time you dialed
into my dream,
"I've got to take a trip
but the airport's closed."
I said, "I'll hang up now
to let someone else take care of you."
Was it then I let you go?

Everyone else touches the dead.
I wear the orchid you sent me.
When the postman rang
I wasn't home.
The orchid lay day after day in its box
until I claimed it.
Vampire, I lifted it out.

You completed your mission.
I don't need to be haunted.
We said goodbye.

Golden Chains

Today cloudy as the steam
from Russian trains
I think of how we're all connected.

Today I find baby birds
who perished in their flight
from the swallow's nest I protected.
I wouldn't let the workers hose it down
but the fledglings died anyway.

I'm not God.

I wish I understood connection:
In your teenage dream
my mother
and you
and I
all drove cars
hooked together with golden chains.

I wish I understood
how comets let down the trapeze
that every once in a while
we can swing high enough
to catch that glimpse of past, present, and future
all at once
to see we're connected.

When you worked in New York
I gave you a party.
I took your friends to the Russian Tea Room.
We ordered herring and caviar.
Steam from the samovar
made me think of generations
of stories:

my dream after you were born
when I stood at the base
of our apartment with your grandmother
and looked up, up, seeing above me
all your stories.

Fellowship

It's almost New
Year's Eve
and I haven't done my life yet,
still stuck on that year
as a graduate student
on fellowship.

My German roommate
taught me to make glu wine
and cook calves' brains.
We invited our professors to parties.
They drank from our toothbrush glasses.
She told me about her town in Germany
where Schiller lived in a tower.

Every time I bought a new dress
she got one like it, smaller.
I took her home with me to Iowa.
She complained my mother's laundry detergent
ruined her sweaters.
Mother said German dyes are inferior.
French sauces disguise bad meat.

Her father was a merchant.
Mine sold lumber.
We deplored commerce.
We would marry artists, writers.
I read Erich Maria Remarque,
sat in on German classes.

My true love, the soldier in Germany,
sent me a compact
with edelweiss
on umber. He scratched in my name.
Delicate
but I was out for big game.

I married the man with posture
who told me I needed an anchor
when what I craved was ballast.
I threw the urine bottle
into the Platte River.
I wasn't pregnant after all.
Too late!
I'd given up my fellowship.
Calamity kept us together eighteen years.

Here it is New Year's Eve
and I haven't caught the sadness
when she came to visit my new marriage.
She used up every fellowship. Fulbright,
Danforth,
now supported herself
as a potter.
At fifty she would go forth.
All these years with a married man
who paid for the abortion.

It's nearly the stroke of twelve.
I'll never get it done.
I'll have to leave it unclosed
like the other episodes.
I took the train through Ulm,
saw her family's motor-work sign,
the town hall
with its procession of elves,
the tower where the poet pined.
I didn't call. Too late.

Highway

Because he was a soldier in Germany
at the time and I fell
in love with graduate school and professors,

I never married my true love.

During one firefly-lit night
in the back seat of his Chevy,
he told me that his family planted
a stand of cottonwoods at the birth
of a son.

I never bore his child
but I looked for that wall of trees
when I drove back to our hometown.
The highway still scrapes
through the room
where I married and divorced
the professor.

I looked for cottonwoods, their seeds blowing
across the road. The field was bare.

Forty years later
I saw the lake by his farm
dredged.
If there were cottonwoods
they are now dead, their lumber
used for chest or cradle,
empty.

Unnamed

My name is not known
but to the pear tree
on Lexington

the forsythia
whipping the Park

the starlings that sing me awake
while the shark moon bottoms out
with the lamps.

Fat snowdrops tamp my forehead
as I fall back into sleep.

My name will be known in the potters' field
where unnamed
children are carried down the ramp—
prisoners bury them, 50¢ an hour.

The sign above the cemetery at Hart Island
reads:

Don't cry for us
we are at peace.

Flying into the Fire

You're a veteran of four wars.
In Vietnam you turned to
your dead co-pilot
and saw the fear still on his face.

When you went home with the body
his mother asked,
"Why wasn't it you instead?"

In Jerusalem a bomb
killed your wife
while she sat with you on the park bench.

Now I fly into the fire.
I have escaped death
too many times,
I won't rest until all the children
have enough to eat.

Pianos around the Cape

At last we found Happy Valley
and the long walkway to the house
my husband's great-great-grandfather
saved from burning in the Civil War.

In amber light,
we traced his family back through twenty
layers of wallpaper adjoining fireplaces
in every room.
During Stoneman's Raid
the slaves hid in chambers behind the hearth.
We laid hands on the worn-down bricks
they used for carving stones.

After the War, the brothers, California bound,
shipped their pianos around the Cape.
The sisters and the mothers filed to the Pacific
Ocean to do their wash.
They dried long skirts on cypress branches.
Cattle ate the cloth for salt.

Pine Cones

With little pain you bear a daughter.
A golden child who loves you
as much as you love her.
She places her head in your lap.
She swings from the pine in a cut-out tire:
all of it meant to be.

Voices tell you the gods are jealous.
You ask, "Jealous of goodness?"
Once the doctor cut a half-moon
in her eardrum.

Children arrive as pine cones.
You hold them on your lap, prickles or no.
The gods are fuming.

Your friends write
her life had meaning.
You see her descend the golden staircase.
The disease attacked her DNA.

People die in this plague,
flies in the eyes of African children.

In her wedding dress she lies
beneath a pine.

Snapped

Acorns so thick we skated through them!
We cracked the buckeye
and the chestnut cask
beneath our boots.
The wooly worm, orange
turned black, augured
for the one-hundred-year's frost.
Farmers predicted ice.

Telephone poles snapped.
No power in the Blue Ridge.
We opened our house,
laid a fire with hickory.
We served black-eyed peas
and grits to kin.
Blizzard turned to sacrament.

That other New Year's
you and I scaled Blowing Rock.
I pressed to drag you back
from the winds that tore you,
until something
in me snapped.
I had to let the snow enfold you.

My Last Poem to Grief

At last I take off my shoes
enter the Blue Mosque
with its six minarets.
You begged me to sail to Istanbul
with you, come to this mosque
where in the days of the Sultan
the attendants all wore blue.
Once-blue carpets covered the tile.
Umber stained-glass windows remain.

All blue.

In my airport dream
I see you passing through security
with your excellent posture.
Your carry my blue suitcase.
I release that baggage now.
We're both pilgrims,
both safe. I send up my poem to grief.

Outside in the Hippodrome, Turks play
on the pipes, offer raki to the tourists.
The cobras rise.
I, Kokopelli,
let the songs burst forth from my haunch.
Poems coil into sweet air
from the Rio Grande to the Bosphorus.

Ivory

Not just any old cracked bar
from the bathroom sink
but brand-new soap
wrapped in hospital blue and white

was offered up
for the ceremony
when they washed out my mouth.

I felt soap soft as cattleya petal on my tongue
before I ever dreamt of the orchid,
alligator pear or elephant tusk world outside
the Iowa snow.

I demanded a baby doll that could piss.
I couldn't let it alone.
"I want her to piss. Piss." Until soap
was the only solution.

In the oral-sex impeachment war
piss lost some punch.
Nothing beats it for fragrant
steaming grate or saffron snow.

I'm proud
that at the age of four I went to the mat
for this word.

Eclipse

While the husband worked
she grew into her redwood house
as in her childhood story
of people who merged with oak
trees.

When she was thirty she awoke to acorns
dropping on her roof.
She knew she would be initiated
into the rite of trees
during the lunar eclipse.

She crept out and spied the tangled
red yarn in the moon.
Bloodlines in the moon.
She ventured one foot into the tree bark.
It yielded and she entered the tree.

She slept there until she heard
her husband chopping wood.
She gave him a basket of red
yarn. He grew plump and one day said,
"This house no longer suits me."

When they moved on
her necklace caught on the pump handle.
Pearls scattered
under the redwood deck.

She wondered if the wagon would bring
her back one day; if the pearls
would have grown into mushrooms.

Single

You always loved the red madrone.
It may well have been the only one
in San Luis Obispo County.
We hiked there through private
property.

At night while my children slept,
you went out
to pee with my collie at dawn, leapt
the fence. When their father took them
for Xmas, you invited me home to Oregon.

Your mother,
only a little younger than me, knitted
warm slippers for my cold feet.
She told me how you children loved to watch
rain spill over the firewood.

I loaned you the station wagon
to interview in the Valley.
After you moved I pulled on boots to visit
the red madrone.
Rain tore off its bark in the sheets.

Occupation

The moon was done up
in knitting needles
in the land where you loved.

You changed your name
when you went to bars. You said
the girls loved you for your kind
eyes. They were starving.

You said she knew
her place.   I didn't
measure up. Not sexy enough,
not implacable enough.

She became my occupation.
I saw her bound up in pink obi.

I went to Japan for myself.
Women surrendered
to me, too.
The old woman scrubbed my back
in the o-furo.

You brought back a fan from Japan
for the girl you would marry.
It smelled of sandalwood
when I snapped it.

Rain Dance

Twenty years of waiting for him
to apologize, to ask me to dance,
I asked him

and we danced at our son's wedding
to his Mexican beauty. Two hours
with mariachis, all night with DJs.
Salsa, meringue, samba, cha-cha-cha.
Even to *Smoke Gets in Your Eyes*,
while the machine threw out smoke.

And on the bronzed California hills,
it began to rain as in the green
corn dance at Zia Pueblo. It rained down
mudheads, koshares, crickets, lightning
bugs and lightning. The Wall
broke into wet crumbling adobe.
Our grandchildren slid down the berm
like salamanders.

And I forgave him,
understood why smoke
got in my eyes, why lovely things die,
why I loved him.
The shine on our children's faces
when they saw us dancing
made me grieve for our estrangement.
Our children, with splits in their heads
like Frankenstein's monster, would not heal,
become whole, until I merged with the other
half of the nucleus. I grieved
that I withheld this peace from them.

And we danced in the rain until dawn
until the bride was green with dollar bills.

Our Four Corners

Whenever there is water
someone is drowning.
　　—Robert Bly

Friends, consider that we have always lived
under the narcosis of water lilies.
This room is the aquarium and we are all dreaming
within it. Remember how our teachers held us
until the sun lit up seaweed in late afternoon?
Afterwards in the castle, bride and groom.
We never questioned our four corners.

When the Buddhist master married us
he said, "You cannot love anyone in this life
you have not loved in your first body
of water." That is why we come in different shapes
and sizes. There is room in the ocean
for the doll, the skull and the anchor.
When you find someone she has always
been there. When you lose someone
he is treading the water near you.

Time Is the Canoe

This morning I woke up
as a blue jay dove into wisteria.
I looked down when a loquat fruit
hit my foot.
Where did spring,
this industry, come from?

Magnolias in water eradicate
musk from library stacks.

I cracked open a Brazilian
story, "The Third Bank." A man
hacks out a canoe and paddles the river
forever, through his daughter's wedding,
his son's rite of passage.
What is the meaning of the canoe?
His sarcophagus?

Time is the canoe.
We climb into our vehicles
leaving the ones who love us yearning.
We go unswerving. We do
what is to be done.

Amber

Try as you might
you can't escape the vessel.
Here we are
popped out in Copenhagen
where men wear top hats.
Skyscrapers carry domes, too.

At the Danish Modern Lutheran
Church, two Mormon missionaries
befriend us.
They usher us down the line-up
of severe apostles.
Peter holds the keys to the kingdom.

Everyone's on a mission.
The Buddhist tourist scurries
to capture the Little Mermaid.
Marble on rock, she sits forever,
back to the sea.

I chase my own passion:
Amber! Resin locked in trees
for fifty-three million years. A mosquito's
pinned down, wings back.
Not a bad way to spend eternity.

The Great Dismal Swamp

Swamp for our meeting place
the Great Dismal
hidden between Carolina & tidewater

Virginia   we were young then
up to cypress knees arched

      black gum root.

When we heard the warbler's call
we slid down Jericho Ditch.

Runaway slaves found freedom:
couples eloped.

No one returns from its heart
of ten thousand years' watery growth
but we found our way home
through the forbidden.

In Silence

The deer glides down Manhattan's
Arrowhead.

In silence, in silence.

Invisible in snow, the deer trots,
leads me down
through our history,
when Powhatan sold Manhattan
and George Washington surrendered
his commission to his troops.

To the ancient marble customs house,
in silence to Ground Zero.

People in black weep by the fences.
Umbrellas over their heads
catch the snow.
The tarnished metal letters stand:
The World Trade Center PATH station.

In silence, in silence.

The deer leads us through the snow.
I am invisible
but not afraid of the dark.

You Can't Turn It Back

Once you start something moving
you can't turn it back.

That painful afternoon
I persuaded my kindergarten
teacher to march the class to the chick-
pea garden. In the morning
it sparkled yellow, blue, lilac and pink.
When we got there, all the blossoms
had withered under heat.

No one would believe me again.

Decades later, I learned the word
ephemeral. Grab it when you can.
And the word *inexorable*. Once set
in motion it won't turn back.
The Model T wasn't going too fast.
Tippy wasn't chasing it
but he got caught

under the wheels. He hightailed
it back to the yard and died
in my arms. I couldn't do anything
but watch it all play out.

That bright morning when my children
and ex drove off for Alaska, the man
who broke up my marriage and I
strolled through a field of chick-peas.
All of a sudden he vanished.

Scared, I discovered him
hiding face down in the vines.
What a jerk. But what has been started
must be played out.

The Vietnamese Princess

One foggy beach night
winding my way back from the prison
through the eucalyptus grove
she flickered in my headlight.
That young woman in odai racing
her motorcycle across the sand
didn't make a sound.
The tails of her garment and black hair
flew behind her as she receded
into fog. This ghost was chasing someone.

In his yarns of the Vietnamese netherworld,
Vi enchanted our class with her doomed life.
When someone had too much rice
it was her destiny to even it out, take a life.
She lived where children sobbed
for their mothers, where mothers
searched for their babes. Once a princess,
she even frightened royalty.

When the fog rolled in, Vi's stories unnerved
me. I requested an officer
to escort me to my pickup.
Vi was a gentle soul. Hard to believe
he murdered his wife.

Gang Wars and Galapagos

When I said, *"Yo soy el interprete"*
the patient took my hand. Healing
happened there and then. I knew
language was the cure. "Your cause
is my cause. Your pain is my mission.
Don't be afraid. You will be heard."

Fidelina sat straight in her immaculate
cotton blouse, washed and ironed
a thousand times. I helped her
with her gown; we filled out the forms.
Growing up she worked in the *milpas*.
Her family could not afford the *cuadernos*
for writing the alphabet.
She never learned to read.

The gang stabbed Fidelina's son outside
the 7-Eleven in Santa Maria.
The police never investigated. Now
she suffers from insomnia and depression.
The doctor took Fidelina's hand.
It's good for a psychiatrist
to watch the *interprete* break down and cry.

In the Galapagos, we walk up to the fuzzy
baby albatross, beak open, waiting for his next
meal. Since we aren't allowed to feed or touch,
the birds don't live with fear.
Without predators the cormorant lost
its ability to fly. And I once believed
flight/fight was the only way to live.

Libido Dreams

Searchlight on
the helicopter
shattered my window

hunting for the Siberian
tiger in my dream. Escaped
from the Moscow
circus, he snapped at a whip,
pulled against the lead
in my left hand.

My right hand guided
a three-eyed dog.
Right side warped
left side healthy and roaring.

Searchlight
since the last dream:

I met an anaconda in the forest
who tried to lure me back
but I promised to attend the gala.

At dinner I shrieked
at the anaconda settled in my lap,
coiling up to the red wine.

Champagne Toast
for Hugh

We knew elegance
was holding champagne
but we favored red wine,
the color of our dancing shoes.

We turned afternoons
and evenings into glamour,
noses to the host.
Strange that we look so alike.

Secrets underlie the instant
of light on water,
the water striders on pontoons.

We seize our glasses
toasting on the edge of what
rises and drifts down-river.

The tongue dissolves.

All we need is a breeze
to lift us to our bed
overlooking the forest.
We perished for the city,
the crowd we thought we knew.

Kestrel

Dammit! I couldn't send you a Val-
entine this year; I drove you . . . I mean
your ashes to Yosemite.

When I saw you in your mask
I swerved into the fence post
but you perched again and

again, kestrel beside crow on the high
tension wire, everywhere along the Grapevine.
In the lodge, too, the kachina figure

of the kestrel said endurance.
The turtle on your garment said energy
from underground. In your codicil

you requested Delphi, the navel of the world.
Sure, I would chew those laurel
leaves for you, shimmy down the crevice

and screech my prophecy, "You'll fry in Hell
for leaving me!" Fat lot of good that would do.
So I hike . . . unsteady on the ice to

Bridal Veil Falls, throw a fistful of you
into the mist. My nostrils catch grit
flying back. Not bad.

Kestrel's message from underground:
Endurance. I couldn't get rid
of you if I tried.

Be mine.

The New House

We'll turn over new leaves.
Oak floors will be polished,
the oak table will gleam.

We'll sow the yard in clover
I'll build hives for the bees
hutches for rabbits
runs for chukars.

The oak table will gleam.

I'll tie up raspberry vine
with old silk hose
and mulch the roses with peat.

In this house we'll live forever
tablets behind our beds:
Here lie two grown children
with children of their own.

Oak floors will be polished,
the oak table will gleam.

Marine Layer

With a stiff neck
I pray for fog to lift.
At 10:00 the sun comes out:
my favorite time to call you.

Hi Mom, just a minute. Let me hook up.

I know the routine.
First saline, then foscarnate
that leaves you without an appetite.
I feel it pour into you
like breast milk.
I'm grateful. You're alive.

Good-bye. I feel so good when I unhook.

I could go about my day.

Salt of the Earth

A child kicking through the prairie
buffalo grass and cactus
I discovered sculpture that cattle
polished with their tongues.

Salt lick: more delectable than ice
cream, also churned with salt,
more permanent than the blocks
of ice we carried home on the dray.

I used to think that salt of the earth
meant the grim ones,
my ex-husband who on our first
barbeque scolded me when I forgot

salt. That and my leaving him
likely spared him a heart attack.
I should have let salt give me my clue.
Stay away from those who aggravate

your wounds, salt would say. Stick
with those who give life flavor.
I owe my life to salt but now pop
pills to drain it from my heart.

Salt flows back into the sea
where the halibut don't mind
when it seeps into their eyes. It will create us
over and over again from scratch.

They Do Death Right

They do death right
in the South.

"After they wash the corpse
the hair is straight.
I bring in my own hair dryer
and curling iron.
It's the last thing
I can do for my friend."

In the South, the dead
are safe. The traffic pulls
to the side of the road
to honor the funeral procession.

The snake handlers
quote Matthew. "They
who believe in the Lord
will not perish
from the serpent's bite."

They do death right.
At his viewing, my yard-
man who sowed ginseng
and cresie greens for me
wore a brand new pair
of bib overalls.

There was a telephone
among the gladiolas.
The ribbon said, "Jesus called."

They do death right.

Bottom Feeders

Life so overgrown, hard to remember only three years ago Queenie
clear sailing, with her long ivory cape streaming behind.

Her namesake: A Reina Santa Isabel, medieval Portugal, took bread
from the castle to feed the poor. Her husband, Dom Dinis, founded
the University where I studied in Coimbra, walking two miles up crooked
steps to school. He said to Isabel, "Open your cape," and out fell roses.

Queenie was magic too. When she floated by, the lotus bloomed.
Wise, she knew that the lotus flourishes only in filthy water
but one raccoon-masked night she disappeared. I grieved he took
the most majestic one. Bill said, "She was wild. You have to let her go."

Every morning she swam to meet me, but now in the overgrowth
the fish open up like vacuum cleaners. They can't tell
if we're medievalist, ichthyologist or raccoon. In this jungle
we're all reduced to bottom feeders.

Feathers Everywhere

I loved my stained and smelly bathrobe as much as my scrap
of blanket that Grandmother, showing mercy, would rescue
from the trash time after time. That summer the girl at Paso
Robles Park took me to meet her parents in their jalopy,
a cardboard suitcase roped on top. The mother nursed a baby.

Young as I was I understood their poverty. My friend introduced
them as royalty. I understood family then. Next summer in Fresno
I learned how chickens mate, and later about human sex, even
more weird. Feathers everywhere.

Root Beer Float

First time in sixty years I order a root
beer float. I'm old enough to get what I want.

I want to slurp it in private but this man,
construction worker, plops down too.

I slurp. He moves. Good. I ask the soda jerk
for another squirt. I'm old enough.

This construction guy takes out his book
to highlight passages. Sorry I made him move.

Finally, "What are you reading?"
"*A Buddhist Theory of Time and Space.*"

Oh. That's what I wanted to read. I'm old
enough. Another squirt of root beer.

"I hope you enjoy *Time and Space.*"
"Hope as much as you enjoyed your root beer."

One last slurp. Bottom's up.
I've paid my bill.

How Lucky I Am a Late Bloomer

Walking to the English building
after rain
I discover black mushrooms
on the grass with black walnuts.

What a combination!
How lucky I am—a late bloomer.

As long as you're alive
you can always surprise someone.

Right?

When you're dead
even though you've tried to hide
a novel in a Swiss vault
or scrolls in a Swiss cheese
your papers are soon in order.
First time you've ever been organized.

And the last.

So I go on living
in confusion
and bring out four young opossums
on my back after rain.
We scurry to the bulletin board
to scheme about study
in Cambridge, Oxford, or Edinburgh.

Contests!
Submit to the *Virginia Quarterly Review*
share ride to San Francisco.

Ah, my travel agent—
bulletin board of the English department,
life is still before me.

Not Quite Love

Because Eros keeps the heart alive
and I want you
and love to live forever
I not only forgive but celebrate
the cabaret dancer who ran her fingers
over your pate
while I lay wheezing in my berth
with double pneumonia
during our anniversary cruise.
I forgive the other passengers who saw me
falling out of the infirmary, arms full
of antibiotics, elixirs and cotton balls,
the ones who crowed, "Now you can open
your own drug store and by the way
too bad you didn't catch the performance
your husband put on. Great fun but keep
him home."

When the bronchitis let up so I could talk
I inquired why you didn't tell me
and why you weren't there when I was sick.
You said, "There's always that baldheaded guy
in the front row. You said, 'Go out. Have fun.'
I came home. Nothing to tell."

Hell.
Since Eros keeps the heart alive
I accept and celebrate. I've never been sick
again. Not once.

The Beautiful Game

I wanted to write you a poem about the Dordogne where
we could bite into a croissant in the open-air cafe and watch
the brown river flow by the mill houses.

But here I am in Brasil where we spoon down *feijão* with farina
and on the Copacabana drink milk from ice-cold coconuts
that shirtless waiters whack open with a machete.

I wanted to write you a poem about the Tour de France
where we lined up to cheer the cyclists off
as they whizzed past the Bastille,

but here I am in Brasil where we samba in the streets
when we win the World Cup and everyone embraces and kisses.
We're part of the Beautiful Game. I wanted to tell you

about the beauty parlor where I got a chic bob
in Bordeaux. But I'm in Brasil where I have my nails painted
the blue, gold and green of their flag and the gentlemen

get their heads shaved in the style of soccer hero Ronaldinho
while the women have bikini waxes discreetly called *perna inteirna*.
Beauties on Ipanema make Brigitte Bardot look overdressed.

Most of all I wanted to remind you of the taxi driver in Paris
who threw us out, suitcases and all, on the anniversary of Normandy
because we forgot the address of our hotel.

But since I'm in Brasil and the taxi driver nearly kisses my hand
for tipping him two *reais* for the safe trip back from the botanical
garden, I have to face it: I am a child of the New World, a lover

of this country where when slavery was abolished by an act of congress
the people threw roses into the assembly. The American ambassador
gathered them up. He said, "For this, my country had to fight a war."

He Called Me Oatmeal Protestant
for Thomas McGrath

I came to him in nakedness.
I confessed that on the way home
from school I loitered
while the others raced ahead.
He knew.

I slipped into the Catholic Church to trace
my hand in holy water, sniff the incense
and adore the statues.
I only viewed such beauty through the Buddhist
Caves in the *National Geographic*.

He knew I loved beauty and joy
above all else. When that sullen poet compared
me to Doris Day, condemned to happiness
and blondness, he put his arm around me.

"Quit revising," he said, "only God
and Satan are pure."

He knew that joy comes from surviving
the tomb. He said the Irish would rather die
than not fight. Lazarus laughed when Jesus
brought him back to life. Already he could
see death seeping into mine.

I came to him in nakedness.
I learned worldliness. His union protest
blacklisted him in Hollywood.
The Wobbly members in overalls who drove
their campers to hear him in Port Townsend
ate from cans around the fire: his royalty.

He spoke of how our people moaned
as they died from hunger in the potato
famine. During those times Protestants
served us oatmeal on Sunday,
provided we stay on to church.

Who would not convert?
As my poets in prison say:
You can't beat three hots and a cot.

Later my family became Methodist, and obeyed
John Wesley's injunction to do what is shameful,
to visit prisoners and patients in mental hospitals.

Tom McGrath, father and priest, visited all of us.
I came to him in nakedness. When he took
me to bed he called the next day,
early, in time for morning mass.

A Pereira

for Phil and Jackson

A perfect drive from Fresno,
cattle wading through green. Grass parted
oceans through Portuguese dairy farms,

horses forged like horseshoes into mountains.
Good luck all the way! We picnicked in wild-
flowers, faces remembered, names forgotten.

With their fragrance it all came back:
Blue-eyed grass, Cup o' Gold, Clarkia. A stop
at the James Dean monument in Cholame

to consider the inscription: *The young who fall
as blossoms are eternal*. Nearby a biker's
leather jacket read, "Jesus

would have rode a Harley." At home, a glacier
of pear blossoms. My pereira bloomed
while I was gone.

O, let me have one more passionate chance.

Afterword

When I came back from Colombia in 1967, my first book of poems under one arm, my fourth baby cradled in the other, it seemed I would never adjust to New Mexico. Two years later I felt like I could never leave it. Memories I could never have had anywhere else include violent thunderstorms out of clouds that looked like cathedrals, summer roundup on the Lee Ranch, Shalako in Hopi territory, meeting Frank Waters and also Lady Brett from the D.H. Lawrence days. She asked me to read her palm and told me everything I said was true. Her first date was with Winston Churchill, although I did not see that in her palm.

I hated to leave Medellin Colombia, where the sun was as soft as the cheese they peddled in banana leaves, for Albuquerque— the sun a barrel in a rifle. I came to love the desert. It taught me sobriety, to focus my vision.

When I first started *Café Solo* as a dialogue between the Americans, Gene Frumkin helped me select poems. Robert Creeley, whom I knew through my El Paso friend, John Rechy, also brought me into the fold. I met Muriel and Henry Roth, who had come to New Mexico on a D.H. Lawrence Fellowship. He recommended me for the fellowship and I spent a summer in Taos at the Lawrence Ranch. Later I returned for another summer in Taos at the Helen Wurlitzer Foundation, under the direction of Henry Saurwein.

That first drive to California with my children was a wrenching one but I began to understand it held its own beauty: golden hills punctured by black oaks like Kabuki dancers with arms and legs sticking out. I loved California authors, too: Gerald Haslam's essays and stories. I am grateful to him for his Preface to this book; to long-time friend Bill Witherup for contributing to the editing of these poems; to Susan Kelly whom I met in my hometown of San Luis Obispo where she lived for some time, and to photographer Nell Campbell from Santa Barbara and for Nancy Woodard for drawing it all together. Most of all I am grateful for editor John Crawford and his unremitting attention to detail. He calls himself a communist and is really a sweetheart.—Glenna Luschei

Magazine Acknowledgments

Through the forty-five years of the composition of my collected poems I am grateful to the following publishers and ask forgiveness for the ones that I have inadvertently omitted:

American Poetry Review, Antenna, Art/Life, Askew, Blue Mesa Review, "But Is It Poetry?", Café Solo, Calapooya Collage, California State Poetry Quarterly, Caprice, Central, Central Coast Times, Concelabratory Shoehorn Review, Confrontation, Dacotah Territory, DayBreak, The Decade Dance, Earth's Daughters, Fragments, Free Lunch, Gas, Greenfield Review, The Hollins Critic, Hubbub, Hyperion, Interstate, Iris, Kamadhenu, Kayak, Kenyon Review, The Last Cookie, Live Wire Press, Midwest Express Special Editions, Mill Mountain Review, Negative Capability, New Mexico Magazine, New Mexico Review, New Works Review, North Stone Review, Old Crow, Oread, Out of Sight, Painted Bride Quarterly, Parnassus, The Pedestal Magazine, Pembroke, Prairie Schooner, Presa, Quetzal, Raven, Redstart, Rivertalk, Rio Grande Writers Association Chapbooks 4 and 5, Road Apple Review, Salt Creek Reader, Salt River Review, Searchcraft, Snowy Egret, South Dakota Review, Sur, Water Rooster, Whole Notes, Wildflowers, The Windflower Home Almanac of Poetry, and Whole Notes.

About the Author

Glenna Luschei has published the poetry magazines *Café Solo, Solo,* and *Solo Café* for forty-five years. She was a founding member and eventual Chair of the Committee of Small Magazine Editors and Publishers in the nineteen-seventies. She has received a National Endowment for the Arts Fellowship, a D.H Lawrence Fellowship in Taos, New Mexico, an honorary Doctorate of Literature from St. Andrew's Presbyterian College in Laurinburg, North Carolina, and a Master of Life Award from her alma mater, The University of Nebraska. She was named Poet Laureate of San Luis Obispo City and County for the year 2000.

On returning to the United States after years in Colombia in 1963, Luschei determined to start Solo Press and the magazine *Café Solo* as an exchange between Spanish and English poets. Those years were formative for her, working under the guidance of Gene Frumkin and Robert Creeley. She has published in *New Mexico Quarterly; New Mexico Review; Blue Mesa Review;* and *In Company,* published by the University of New Mexico Press. Her inclusions in other anthologies consist of *Chance of a Ghost,* Helicon Editions; *The Sorrow Poems,* University of Iowa Press; *White Ink Poems on Mothers and Motherhood,* Demeter Press, Toronto; *The Geography of Home,* Heyday Press; *Big Bear Republic,* Alcatraz Editions; and *Letters to the World,* Red Hen Press.

Luschei is the author of a number of books, special editions and chapbooks, the most recent books being *Libido Dreams,* Artamo Press, 2007 and *Total Immersion,* Presa Press, 2008. She published an artist book, *Enigmas,* of her translation of Sor Juana Inés de la Cruz, in 2006. She taught for many years at UCLA Arts Reach, Chaplin College at the California Men's Colony, Cal Poly at San Luis Obispo and Atascadero State Hospital. For four years, she was also a panelist for the National Endowment for the Arts. She completed her own studies in Hispanic Languages and Literatures at the University of California, Santa Barbara in December 2005 and was awarded a PhD degree.

She is now an avocado rancher in the Carpinteria Valley. She has served as State Land Use Officer for California Women in

Agriculture and on the Family Services Bureau of the USDA. A bilingual speaker, she interprets for migrant farm workers from Mexico and Brazil.

Books by Glenna Luschei

COLLECTIONS AND CHAPBOOKS
Letter to the North (Papel Sobrante, 1967)
Back into My Body (Thorp Springs Press, 1974)
30 Songs of Dissolution (San Marcos Press, 1977)
Redwoods (San Marcos Press, 1983)
Swimming Suit: a Suite (San Marcos Press, 1983)
Unexpected Grace (Turkey Press, 1984)
Diving through Light (Tiger Stream Press, 1985)
Farewell to Winter (Daedalus Press, 1986)
Bare Root Seasons (Oblong Press, 1990)
Offering the Throat, with Kevin Patrick Sullivan (Solo Press, 1991)
Matriarch (The Smith, 1992)
Cassandra Speaks Up (Ancient Mariners, 1992)
Spirit of Place (Cal Poly Foundation, 1993)
Cities of Cibola and Other Poems (Midwest Express Special Editions, 1993)
Back into My Body (Mille Grazie Press, 1994)
A Near Country, with David Oliveira and Jackson Wheeler
    (Solo Press, 1999)
Water Rooster (Backer Editions, 1999)
Pianos around the Cape (Aspermont Press, 1999)
Shot with Eros (John Daniel and Co., 2002)
Seedpods (Presa Press, 2006)
Libido Dreams (Artamo Press, 2007)
Total Immersion (Presa Press, 2008)

ARTIST BOOKS
Silk & Barbed Wire, with linocuts by Anita Segalman (Solo Press, 1986)
Here, with linocuts by Anita Segalman (Solo Press, 1989)
Wind Machines, with linocuts by Anita Segalman (Solo Press, 2000)

ARTIST BOOKS IN TRANSLATION
Polyphemus and Galatea, Some Lines in Translation, Luis de Gongora
    y Argote, with linocuts by Anita Segalman (Solo Press, 1995)
Enigmas, Sor Juana Ines de la Cruz, with linocuts by Anita Segalman
    (Solo Press, 2006)